FAMILIES
ARE DIFFERENT

FAMILIES
ARE DIFFERENT

written and illustrated by Nina Pellegrini

Holiday House / New York

Library of Congress Cataloging-in-Publication Data
Pellegrini, Nina.
Families are different / written and illustrated by Nina
Pellegrini.—1st ed.
p.   cm.
Summary: An adopted Korean girl discovers that her classmates have
different types of families.
ISBN 0-8234-0887-6
[1. Family—Fiction. 2. Adoption—Fiction. 3. Korean Americans–
–Fiction.]   I. Title.
PZ7.P3635Fam   1991
[E]—dc20   90-22876
CIP
AC

Hello, my name is Nico. Actually, Nicola, but everyone calls me Nico. I live in a large town with my family. I have a mother and father, a big sister, and a dog.

My sister's name is Angelica.
We call her Angel, but if
you ask me, she's no angel.
Sometimes she drives me
BONKERS!

We fight a lot, but we still love each other—TONS!

Angel is teaching me how to read,

but I don't always pay attention.

Angel looks a lot like me. We are both adopted.
We came from Korea when we were babies.
Korea is a country on the other
side of the world.

Sometimes we wear
our special Korean
outfits.

First came Angel. Then, four years later, I came. My mom and dad and sister met me at the airport—but not my dog.

My dog's name is Buster. He doesn't look like me,
but sometimes we have the same hairdo.

He gives me lots of slurpy kisses. Buster is one of my best friends.

I have four best friends, counting Angel and Buster.

My other best friends are Molly and Anna.
We go to kindergarten together, where we play for
most of the day. We are six years old now.

My mom and dad are really old. You have to count to above thirty to get to their age. I love them a lot! I hug, hug, hug them, and give them lots of kisses.

They don't look like me, either. They both have blue eyes and wavy hair. That's because I'm adopted. I grew in someone else's belly, but my mom and dad are the ones who promised to love and take care of me forever.

At first, I didn't think it was strange that I looked different. Then, for a while, it bothered me because Molly and Anna look like their moms and dads. I wanted to be just like them.

Sometimes I even felt angry or sad.

I would hear mothers talking to each other and they
would say, "Oh, your baby looks just like you." That
made me feel different, too.

Then I talked to my mom about it. She told me that there are different kinds of families. She said that they are glued together with a special kind of glue called *love*.

So I started looking around, and this is what I saw:

One of the kids in my class looks like his
dad, but not like his mom.

One boy has a sister and a mom for a family,
but not a dad.

There is a big family who are all related. They look alike, even their dog, Sparky.

And there is also a medium-sized family who all look different, even though they're related, too.

There is a very small family of a little girl and her dad.

And there's a girl whose parents are divorced.

There is a boy who lives with
his sister and his grandmother
and grandfather.

My sister has a friend who lives with her father, her
stepmother, and her younger half-sister.

And there is even a family that has one kid who grew in his mom's belly, and one kid who was adopted. There sure are a lot of different families.

Now I don't think I'm strange at all. I'm just like

everyone else . . . I'm different!

And boy oh boy, my family must be stuck together

with strong glue

because . . .

There's sure a TON of love around here!